COMPROMISE OR CONFRONTATION

ISABEL BURK MAZZENGA

Compromise or Confrontation

DEALING WITH THE ADULTS IN YOUR LIFE

DRAWINGS BY ANNE CANEVARI GREEN

FRANKLIN WATTS
NEW YORK LONDON TORONTO SYDNEY 1989
A VENTURE BOOK

Library of Congress Cataloging-in-Publication Data

Mazzenga, Isabel Burk.
Compromise or confrontation : dealing with the adults in
your life / by Isabel Burk Mazzenga.
p.   cm.—(A Venture book)
Bibliography: p.
Includes index.
Summary: Discusses how to develop good communication
skills to negotiate with the adults in your life.
ISBN 0-531-10805-8
1. Children and adults—Juvenile literature.   2. Parent and
child—Juvenile literature.   [1. Interpersonal relations.
2. Communication.]   I. Title.
HQ772.5.M39   1989
306.874—dc20   89-5711   CIP   AC

Thanks to my supportive husband, Jerry Mazzenga; my mother, Daisy Burk; Harriet and Len Goodwin; and Marian Wood; who encourage and inspire all my literary efforts. Special recognition to my daughter Heather Mazzenga, her friend Sherri Levinson, and Ken Packer, who patiently and carefully reviewed this book during its formative stages.

Warmest appreciation to Wally Wood, who hired me, encouraged me, and "showed me the ropes" as I began my journalism career.

A note of gratitude to all of my students at Hilltop Intermediate School in Nyack, and at Suffern Junior High School: keep up the great work as you move toward your successful futures!

For my husband, Jerry, and
daughters, Heather and Andrea,
who fill my life with love

CONTENTS

CHAPTER

WHO ARE YOU?

Do you know this riddle? An injured boy lies on the operating room table, ready for surgery. The surgeon lifts the sheet, sees the boy, and cries, "I can't operate on this boy—he's my son!" The boy's father manages a store. His grandfather has retired to the country. So what's the relationship between the boy and the doctor?

BALANCING YOUR ROLES

The surgeon is his mother! Like the mother in this story, you have different roles. You're the child of your parents and a brother or sister to the other children in your family. Plus you're a classmate to all the students in your class, and teammate to the members of your sports team.

You're also a grandchild to your grandparents, student to your teacher, friend to your friends, customer to your local store, and a viewer or listener to television or radio stations. In addition you could be a niece or nephew, cousin, tutor, or

helper. You have quite a lot of relationships to carry on at one time!

And for each relationship, you have different responsibilities. You work with, care for, help, and listen to your friends. As a student, you attend school, listen during lessons, do homework, and learn new skills and information.

In your role as team member, your teammates expect you to work hard, play your best, and cheer them on. As a child to your parents, you do chores in your house, help family members, plan and enjoy activities.

Because of all your roles, different people relate to you in different ways. Marilyn's older sister, Dee, for example, won't allow twelve-year-old Marilyn to borrow her cassette player. Dee thinks Marilyn is a "pesty little sister" who breaks her stuff.

But Grandma Rose knows when she asks Marilyn for help, Marilyn is always there on time and ready for action. To Grandma Rose, Marilyn is a reliable, good-natured granddaughter.

The boy who sits in front of Marilyn in school doesn't tease her anymore. He's found out that Marilyn answers him back so cleverly he feels foolish.

Marilyn's next-door neighbors have asked her to water their plants while they're away on vacation next week. Marilyn often plays with their three-year-old, and they feel she would be a trustworthy caretaker.

Each of these people sees Marilyn differently and treats her differently. She has a different reputation and relationship with each of them in her everyday roles. Yet she's the same Marilyn inside!

Every day you count on people fulfilling their roles, and you know that many people count on you too. You depend on your parents to provide the necessities like a safe home and regular meals. They depend on you to do your homework and help out around the house.

Actually, you and your parents expect many other people to do their jobs: deliver the mail, broadcast radio and television, run the stores, grow the food, and so on. We're links in a giant chain, cooperatively shifting and changing.

Your roles change too. As you grow, you develop new interests, new projects, and new needs. And you assume duties that match your growing abilities.

Sometimes you develop these on your own. Brendan has been fascinated with skateboarding for the past two years. From the time he received a skateboard for his tenth birthday, he's worked hard at developing his skills in the sport.

Brendan started by mastering basics learned from friends. Then he tried new techniques and tricks he learned from magazines and television. Because he's become such an expert, his friends and lots of other kids watch him and ask for advice. They copy his moves and admire his style.

Brendan's proud of his skills, but he realizes his responsibility to others by teaching and practicing safety rules as he skateboards.

As you already know, growing up also means more responsibility at home. Sara's mom wants her to help with the grocery shopping, keep an eye on her baby brother, and run errands. Sara also has to pick up her own dirty laundry, straighten out her dresser drawers, and make her bed every day.

Jesse sets and clears the dinner table, takes out the garbage, dries dishes, shovels snow, and straightens up his room.

You haven't always been able to perform these duties. When you were in kindergarten, your parents woke you up, helped you dress, made your breakfast, and sent you off to school. Now you may set your own alarm, select clothes and dress yourself, have a bite to eat, gather your books, and go to school. Mom knows you can take care of yourself for daily activities. If you need help you'll ask.

You're changing to take on the roles you want and to meet the roles you're assigned.

These changes didn't all happen at once. Little by little, you're growing wiser, more competent, more tolerant. You try harder, learn your lessons, and succeed more often.

Maybe you feel it before anybody else. You're eager for new challenges, but the adults in your life don't agree. Perhaps they don't know how hard you're working to learn new skills. Or they may only see you as a child, and they don't yet appreciate your other, more responsible roles.

Marilyn wants her sister to let her borrow her cassette player. She has her eye on Dee's tape collection too. But Dee doesn't see how responsible Marilyn has become. How can Marilyn show Dee that she's trustworthy? What suggestions would you give her?

GROWING TOWARD ADULTHOOD

Right now your body is preparing for an exciting new role: adulthood. You've noticed changes in your body, and you feel different too.

You're bigger and more mature than you were at six, seven, or eight. You don't really look like a child anymore. Your body is growing up, going through a time of changes called puberty.

Everyone grows at a different rate. Carole was the first girl in her class to menstruate and the first to wear a bra. Although her parents were proud of her, she felt embarrassed to be so different from her friends. Many of the girls asked her questions about her body, and she didn't quite know how to deal with their curiosity.

On the other hand, you may know someone like Felix. He was the shortest, slimmest boy in the sixth grade. While many of his friends were growing taller and developing muscles, Felix had not yet begun his growth spurt. He worried a lot because he still looked more like a boy than a teenager. But over the summer, he began to grow. By winter, Felix had grown over two inches and discovered some dark hairs on his body too. He was very relieved to see these changes.

It's normal to wonder about your body. You think about how tall you'll be and what kind of body shape you'll have. When you notice your body growing and changing, it may not feel comfortable for a while. Sometimes you need to get used to longer arms and legs, a slimmer waist, bigger feet. You may feel very nervous about taking off your clothes in the locker room. And you might find yourself looking at your classmates, comparing their bodies and shapes to your own. Some will probably be bigger and more developed than yours; others may appear younger and less grown up.

As your body changes, you also wonder about your future. What's it like to be a woman? What's it like to be a man? Will I enjoy it? Will I know how to act? Can I handle it?

You may begin to think about the future, building an enjoyable fantasy life about adulthood. Some young people dream about a car they may want to buy, a new house they might own, an exciting job they might have. Others imagine their future husband or wife, maybe even their children!

It's fun to pretend this way, and it helps you prepare for the future. Even though you know you can't totally live your fantasy life, it's healthy to enjoy your daydreams. Some people use these dreams to help them choose goals and activities for their adult life. In fact, the most successful people in the world have said that their achievements began with a dream. Hard work, talents and skills helped make the dream come true.

ROLE MODELS

Puberty is a time when you begin to fit into your new roles. In fact, you gather information about these roles every day.

When you watch television, you see examples of men and women working, playing, laughing, learning about the world, helping others. Are these shows realistic? Do the people you know behave like the characters on TV?

In their drive to maturity, many young people "try on" roles by talking, walking, looking, or behaving like someone they admire. We call these people *role models*, and they may be relatives, friends, movie stars, television actors, or musicians.

Ken enjoyed pitching for his seventh grade team. He wore his baseball cap tilted just like his favorite pitcher. Last month he read on the sports page that this pitcher's lucky meal was meatballs and eggs. Guess what Ken likes to eat before every game?

Hairstyles follow the same pattern. When Shana went to the beauty salon, she brought along a picture from the latest *Teen* magazine. She asked the hairdresser to cut her hair to look like a famous teenage actress. Shana wanted to be beautiful just like the actress she admired.

You get ideas about men and women from books, magazines, and newspapers. Music, movies, commercials, theater, and art present people of both sexes too. Some of these show men and women doing things that may seem perfectly normal to you. You may not accept or believe some of the other views, however. And that's fine.

Everyone has his or her own idea of what it means to be *masculine,* like a man, and *feminine,* like a woman. You've been practicing for these roles since you were little.

Childhood toys may give a clue to developing masculine and feminine roles. Some young boys enjoy dunking a basketball when they're only two years old. Others prefer to "cook" with clay in a play kitchen.

You'll find toddler girls who rock a baby doll to sleep, and little girls who roll toy trucks in the sand. Many children play with action toys, while others prefer quiet scribbling and music. These youngsters are enjoying roles and experiences that will help them shape their future.

Look at the family members you know. Matt's stepfather vacuums the house, cooks dinner on Saturdays, and changes baby Diana's diapers. Matt noticed that his dad never did those chores. His dad preferred to do woodworking or gardening.

Or maybe your mom is like Cindy's mom. She enjoys working with computers and learning about fixing her car. Her mom goes bowling once a week with her friends. As for housework, Cindy and her brother try to keep their rooms neat, and they all pitch in to clean on the weekend.

Selecting your clothes, decorating your room, caring for your pets and possessions, and building your friendships are all steps toward understanding your new role as an adult man or woman.

You probably won't feel comfortable with your new role right away, especially when you're with a member of the opposite sex. If you're a boy, you might not know what to say or how to act with a girl. If you're a girl, you might have the same trouble with a boy.

You might find that you can't act normally in these situations. You might begin to talk very loudly or laugh a lot. Perhaps you'll start wiggling your foot or chewing your gum faster than usual. Or you might get physical, pushing your friends and slapping them on the back.

If you really like the other person, you might not be able to talk with him or her at all. You might feel flushed and sweaty, or lose your voice. You may feel awkward and uncomfortable whenever you're together.

It takes time to get used to adolescence. Even though you think all other teenagers are finding it easy, they all go through this "awkward stage."

Growing comfortable with your role also means making decisions about activities. Sometimes people you know may not understand your choices. Lila preferred softball games over ballet lessons. She often joined the boys when they played ball out in the street. Her older sister Kim teased her, saying she wasn't "ladylike."

Rob has enjoyed playing the piano and performing since he was in the second grade. His family moved when he began the sixth grade. Many of his new classmates laughed at his musical ability.

At first, Rob stopped his piano lessons. Then he realized he didn't have to change. He could do the things that made him happy. Rob taught himself the latest tunes and had a good time playing for his family and friends. The school music director heard about Rob's talent and asked him to play with the chorus for the Spring Show. Rob's classmates aren't laughing any more.

FIND YOUR OWN WAY

You've probably noticed fads in your school. In Mark's class, everyone wore buttons and badges on their jackets. When Mark's brother sent him some college buttons to wear, all his friends asked for one. Mark didn't mind being copied because his brother told him that people usually copy things they like.

You may join the latest fad, whether it's ripped jeans or half shirts. Maybe you're glad you can look just like everyone else; maybe you like the way you look in the latest style.

When your friends try something new, they usually ask you to join in too. You like your friends, you enjoy their company, and you want people to know that you're part of a special group. So you think it over. You want to wear the same ID bracelet, fashion watch, denim jacket, or baseball cap. This doesn't make you weak or unimaginative. You're just expressing yourself.

Sometimes you don't go along with the crowd. Perhaps you're not interested or your parents don't allow it. Maybe you think some fads are ridiculous. Or you just prefer to act as an individual.

It's not always easy to "do your own thing" and

be different. You might be a little confused by your feelings, not sure what to do in some situations.

Your family and even your closest friend may not understand your need to be different. Friends may try to persuade you to change your mind. They often want you to join what they're doing. We call this *peer pressure.*

Peer pressure takes many forms. Stephen, David, and Ryan were laughing in the back of the school bus. David took an apple out of his lunch bag and threw it at a passing car. Ryan thought this was so funny that he opened up his lunch, found some cookies, and threw them at people on the street.

As the bus passed a busy intersection, both boys urged Stephen to throw some food at people waiting for the light to change. Stephen said no. He didn't want to hurt anybody or be part of any of their stupid tricks. David and Ryan tried to make Stephen change his mind. They were mad when Stephen wouldn't join them. When they arrived at school, they called Stephen "sissy" and "chicken."

Jeanette unexpectedly found herself in an uncomfortable situation one day. Randy, the boy she liked, asked if he could study with her after school. She agreed excitedly. On the way home, it occurred to her that her mother would be angry if she knew that Jeanette had been alone in the apartment with Randy. She decided not to mention it.

Jeanette fixed a snack for herself and Randy. After some shy moments, they began to talk and laugh. At 4:30 she sharpened pencils and got some paper. Randy began to laugh.

"I don't want to study yet, do you?" Randy picked up her hand and looked into her eyes. "I want to get to know you better. Why don't we talk in your room?" he asked, standing up. Jeanette suddenly realized that Randy wasn't interested in school work at all. He had something much more personal in mind.

"I'd like to get a head start on the math problems, Randy," Jeanette said. What should I do next, she wondered.

"We can do math in a little while. What's the matter? Don't you like me?" he asked softly, stepping very close to her.

Jeanette's mind began to race. She liked him enough to kiss him (she'd kissed him a million times in her dreams already), but she felt uncomfortable about what might happen after they kissed for a while. She definitely didn't want to turn him off, but she needed some protection in case things went too far.

"My mom'll be home in five minutes, Randy." Jeanette smiled. "She's tired after work, and she usually expects me to finish my homework quickly so I can help fix dinner and clean up the kitchen. Why don't you stay for dinner?"

Randy shook his head. He gathered up his books, saying he'd call her after dinner for the math problems. After he left, Jeanette felt weak and confused. She was glad he went home, but didn't know if he'd ever want to see her again.

People may use peer pressure in other ways, offering you favors of friendship, pleading, or getting angry when you don't agree or join in. Has something like this ever happened to you?

It can be difficult to say no to your friends, especially when they work hard to make you say yes. But it's important for you to feel comfortable making decisions. As you grow older, you'll be making more and more of your own decisions.

As time passes, you will develop and accept your role as a man or woman. Experience helps you sort out your feelings and assume responsibilities. You'll continue to change, learn new skills, and shape your personality.

You are experimenting with roles, attitudes, behaviors, and feelings. You may be happy with some of these new ideas, and you'll soon find out which ones make you uncomfortable.

Lots of people are rooting for you: your parents, relatives, neighbors, teachers, coach, and scout and club leaders. They can offer you help and support. They've had a lot of experience in difficult situations.

You can ask for their suggestions as you climb the ladder to maturity. Sometimes stories about their teenage years may sound familiar to you, although their world and their life-style weren't quite like yours.

Talk to adults when you find yourself at a dead end. They may not agree with everything you do, but you'll find many will be willing to help when you need it.

Look ahead a little. You're on the right track.

"Don't touch my stuff again!" Stefanie yelled, grabbing the books away from seven-year-old Paul.

She locked the bathroom door and looked through the notebook pages carefully. "Thank goodness I didn't leave any important notes inside!" she sighed.

Stefanie really needed more privacy. And she didn't need her nosy little brother blabbing her personal business to the entire neighborhood.

She was still upset at dinnertime. She picked at her food and frowned. Stefanie hardly looked at her mother or brother.

Paul never knew what to expect from his sister these days. Sometimes she'd hug him and help with his homework. Other times she'd call him names or burst into tears. Mother called her moody. Paul just didn't understand what had happened to his friendly sister.

After dinner, Paul came to talk with Stefanie.

"I was just trying to help, Stef, honest. Mom asked me to clear our stuff off the kitchen table," he explained softly.

... AND THIS BULLETIN JUST IN FROM BRIAN'S ROOM ... HIGH PRESSURE SYSTEM MOVING IN ... CRABBINESS ALERT TONIGHT AND INTO TOMORROW ... OCCASIONAL STORMS ... 75% CHANCE OF MOODINESS ....

ANNE CANEVARI GREEN 89

Looking at his pleading face, Stefanie realized it wasn't the first time she had exploded over nothing. She didn't know what was wrong, but she felt funny about it. Has something like this ever happened to you?

EMOTIONS AND YOUR BODY

Lots of young people find their emotions changing as they grow up. You experience new sensations that you don't recognize and can't explain. Or you may react differently to some everyday situation.

You may be surprised by how you feel, but this is normal. As your body changes during puberty, your emotions change too. Many emotional changes are related to your body's physical changes. During puberty, your body chemistry changes a great deal because of *hormones*.

Hormones are chemicals inside your body. These chemicals help your body manage its operations. Hormones are controlled by your brain and some important glands. Many of these chemicals change several times a day. Others change according to your body's needs. A few hormones rise and fall on a monthly schedule.

These natural variations in chemical levels affect your mood and behavior, how you feel and act. A series of rapid emotional responses can cause noticeable changes in your body, brought about by hormones.

When you're under stress, for instance, hormones can cause you to talk faster. Your muscles become tense, your heart pounds, you start to sweat. You're more likely to lose your temper. You might even scream or cry unexpectedly.

Even more amazing, you're likely to find that

you react differently to some ordinary occurrence. This is what happened to Stefanie. In short, you may be a little unpredictable to yourself and to others—and that's normal.

WHAT'S GOING ON?

Some days you may be surprised at how strong your feelings and your responses are. As your body matures, you'll find your emotions get mixed up occasionally. You may feel ridiculous or out of place in some situations.

When Drew heard some bad news, for example, he began to giggle. He found he couldn't control his emotions properly, and that upset him. Being angry with himself only made his giggling worse. He felt confused, out of control, and embarrassed. Have you ever felt this way?

Like Drew, you'll probably find yourself feeling several emotions at once. It could happen when you're alone, with your family and friends, or even in school.

Maybe you'll have trouble sorting out your feelings. Or perhaps you won't take it too seriously, and laugh at yourself a little.

TIME FOR YOURSELF

Todd began to spend a lot more time alone this year. He liked to listen to the radio and talk on the phone to his friends. Sometimes he would sketch a little or read mystery stories. He put a sign over his bed, Do Not Disturb, so his family wouldn't interrupt him. He wanted to be alone.

He didn't really understand it, but Todd felt upset a lot of the time. He found himself answering his parents back loudly, starting arguments, picking fights with his brother. He really wasn't angry with anybody in particular. Todd just felt uncomfortable being with anyone but his very closest friend. He hated sharing the bedroom with his brother; sometimes he just needed to be completely by himself.

Perhaps you've been staying by yourself a lot too. Actually, your need for privacy makes sense. While your body is undergoing major changes, you need time to get used to the "new you" taking shape. Being alone helps you focus on yourself and learn to deal with your life and your problems.

This transformation could take several years to complete, but that doesn't mean you'll always feel like this. You'll find yourself becoming gradually more relaxed as you get used to the new you.

You'll probably find it harder to keep yourself under control on the days when you've been under stress. Sometimes lots of things go wrong all at once, and you can feel like you'll never see the end! Everyone feels like this occasionally, although it's more common during puberty.

GETTING A GRIP

How can you handle these emotional conflicts?

1. Begin by acknowledging your feelings. You have so many feelings at one time, and they're all part of you.

Everyday feelings include love, hate, jealousy, loneliness, embarrassment, joy, fear, and many others. The mixture changes constantly. Check this list and see which of these emotions you've experienced:

sad	happy	patient
afraid	affectionate	brave
loving	bored	lonely
confused	angry	resentful
guilty	embarrassed	nervous
frustrated	shy	worried
ashamed	disgusted	hateful
jealous	silly	disappointed

Your emotions don't make you a good or bad person. Feelings express what's inside of you; they're not a judgment about you.

2. Learn to accept your feelings as a natural part of life. Some feelings change fast, and you know how confusing that can be. One minute you're happily singing harmony with your friends. A moment later you're incredibly angry with yourself for missing a note.

Almost everyone in the world has experienced this sensation. It helps if you remember that you're not stuck with a particular set of emotions. No matter how upset you feel, it will eventually pass.

Not so sure? Well, think back to your early school experiences. Do you recall your frustration as you tried to tie your shoes? Or your first efforts at printing your name? Did your instrument sound like music the first week you took lessons?

You probably felt clumsy, stupid, embarrassed, tired. At the time you may have thought, "I'll never learn!" Look again: you've come a long way. And you don't feel bad anymore, either. You're proud of your accomplishments and you're a capable human being.

3. Express your emotions appropriately. When you're sad you can cry. When you're happy, laugh.

These simple, short-term feelings appear and disappear quickly with no major damage.

Suppose you get upset by your feelings? How can you express yourself and feel better?

Josh admired Alicia, a girl at his church. When Alicia's family moved to a new neighborhood, he wrote to her and called occasionally. But his father told him he was too young to ask Alicia out on a date. Even worse, his father teased him about his crush on Alicia, calling it "puppy love."

Josh was hurt, angry, and embarrassed. He'd expected his father to understand and respect his feelings.

Sitting on his bed. Josh thought about how he could get back at his father. Just then, his friend Eric called up. Josh pulled the telephone into the closet and told Eric about his feelings. When Eric said he understood how he felt, Josh laughed. No one could understand, he thought.

But Eric explained that he'd had a similar experience with his mother. Parents don't always realize they're hurting their kids, Eric found out. He suggested that Josh talk to his dad and tell him how he felt.

The next morning, Josh joined his dad at breakfast. He told his father how hard it was to talk about Alicia and his problem. He needed ideas from his father, not jokes.

His father apologized for making fun of Josh. He did not mean to hurt Josh's feelings. He wanted Josh to realize that everyone has these experiences. Josh laughed as his father told a story about *his* first crush on a girl, back in the fifth grade.

Josh wasn't angry anymore. He expressed his feelings in a positive manner and took action to change the situation, too.

LOOK AT YOUR REACTIONS

After your next blowup, take the time to cool down and think things over. When you examine the situation, you'll find it easier to explore your reactions. You may even find a pattern to the blowups.

Most days Gina let things slide, not reacting to comments or jokes about her body. At 5 foot, 7 inches and 170 pounds, she knew she wasn't the slender model type.

Her mother picked at her constantly, handing her magazines about diet and criticizing how she dressed. Gina just tuned out.

When the gym teacher asked her to stay after class a minute, Gina was afraid she'd get the same treatment from her. She didn't give Mrs. Lynd a chance to talk; she started to cry, telling Mrs. Lynd she was tired of being picked on about her weight.

Mrs. Lynd didn't understand why Gina was so upset. She hadn't even said anything! She had been watching Gina play during gym, and she wanted to encourage Gina to try out for the basketball team next semester. But Gina didn't want to hear about it. They both left upset.

That night while Gina did her homework, she thought about Mrs. Lynd. Of all her teachers, Mrs. Lynd had been the most understanding about Gina's feelings toward her body. Mrs. Lynd took the time to show Gina several new exercises for her waist, and encouraged her to participate in more team activities. She reminded Gina to expect some changes in her body during the next few years.

Gina really liked Mrs. Lynd. So why did she act the way she did?

Thinking back, Gina decided she was really reacting to her mother's nagging. She didn't give

Mrs. Lynd a chance to speak because she thought the teacher would criticize, the way her mother always did. But that wasn't fair to Mrs. Lynd. She decided to talk to Mrs. Lynd after lunch.

There are times in your life when you will overreact in a particular situation. Adults do this too. Sometimes this happens because you're upset over something totally different. You might "take out" your anger on someone else.

This kind of anger can build up over time. If you're dealing with a difficult family situation, such as parents divorcing or an alcoholic parent or grandparent, take a moment to think about your feelings. Does your anger sometimes slip out at the wrong time?

Or perhaps you're very tired, hungry, or dealing with some kind of pain. Physical needs often affect your emotions and communication with others.

When you feel that you can't work or play properly because something is bothering you, it's a good idea to slow yourself down. Take a little time to think and to let your body rest.

You may find it helpful to talk about your problem with someone you can trust. Talk to an understanding friend, a parent, favorite cousin, or teacher.

A drink or a light snack can break up some of your tension and give you energy. Then you'll be refreshed and ready to continue with a more positive attitude.

When you take the time to consider your actions, you learn about yourself and your relationships with other people. You're showing concern for other people's feelings, and becoming more responsible for your relationships.

PLANNING FOR
BETTER RELATIONSHIPS

You can stop some problems before they start.

Sometimes you can't look ahead to events, so you can't avoid the results. But experience shows that most difficulties build slowly over a period of time. If you act to resolve minor annoyances in the beginning, you can avoid many major blow-ups at the end.

That doesn't mean you can control what happens. You can't change other people, and you can't dictate how your parents, adults, or friends will act. As a responsible person, however, you can take some steps to keep conflicts to a minimum.

Learn to solve your problems creatively. First, try to pinpoint the problem. What's happening here? How can you find out more about it? Can you talk with a teacher, friend, relative, neighbor, or coach? Get more information so you can make an informed choice.

Then try to imagine all the possible solutions, no matter how silly some may seem. You can even make a list. Look at each idea and try to think of positive and negative points about each. How would each of these affect your problem? Are you comfortable with this idea? Could it affect other areas or people in your life, as well?

Finally, select the solution which best fits the situation and will serve your needs. Decide how you'll make the changes, and after you've tried it out, rate your choice. Did your plan work? Do you need to change your approach? Do you need more information to find new solutions?

This "decision-making" method works well for a lot of young people and adults. You'll find that you can use it in so many ways.

You can try this approach when you're involved in a school project, when you're fighting with your parents, or when you've broken up with a good friend or favorite group of friends.

During the first few weeks of junior high school, Heather felt lost. Making her way around the confusing building, changing classes, and gulping down lunch made her feel tense. Even worse, she had no friends in her major subject classes.

Monday afternoon her science project partner, Marian, told her she was giving a party Saturday night. Heather didn't know her very well, but she knew how popular Marian was. Heather held her breath as Marian asked if she was free to come. Without hesitating, she happily accepted.

Heather hummed all the way home, floating on the clouds. Her first junior high party! What a great chance to meet lots of other kids and have some fun. She rushed home and called Siobhan, her closest friend, to tell her the news.

"I've heard a little about Marian's parties," Siobhan told her. "My cousin went once and he says she invites much older guys who drink and smoke marijuana."

"What do her parents say?" asked Heather.

"Her parents travel a lot. They're not always home on weekends. Her sister's a senior who spends most of her time with her boyfriend. So big-shot Marian opens up her house for these wild parties," Siobhan said.

Shocked, Heather tried to swallow the lump in her throat. She'd love to meet some older guys, but she wasn't so sure she wanted to be at a party with lots of beer and stuff. And the more she thought about it, she realized that if she went, they'd probably expect her to drink or smoke too.

After dinner, Heather settled down for some serious brain activity. Using the decision-making model, she defined her problem: Should she go to Marian's party or not?

She summarized all the facts she had at hand. She knew that Marian was very popular with a large number of both male and female friends. And these kids brought alcohol and marijuana to Marian's parties.

Next, Heather listed all her alternatives and considered the consequences of each one. She could decide to go to the party. Heather tried to imagine herself at the party, thinking about all the good and bad points. She could get to know lots of new people and become part of a group. She was curious to meet some new boys.

On the other hand, who would she talk with? What would she talk about? What would she do if they offered her a drink or some marijuana? Suppose she got drunk? Or scared? How would her parents react if they found out?

More input needed, she decided, and so she called two friends to ask advice. Both girls told her the same thing: she could go but leave early if she felt uncomfortable. Or, they suggested, she could make up an excuse for staying home. She could get sick, or have to babysit, or go out of town.

Heather thought about it for a long time. Then she considered the alternative, refusing Marian's invitation. This might be embarrassing. Worse yet, Marian could become angry and make Heather miserable at school.

Using the decision-making method helped Heather to sort through her ideas. She explored possibilities and evaluated the results. And she decided not to go, because she felt it wasn't right for her at this time. She fell asleep, relieved that she'd come to a decision.

CHOOSE YOUR TIME

Using your skills to make a wise decision will certainly improve your relationships. To avoid further conflicts, try this simple trick: learn to anticipate trouble before it starts. Why step into the mud if you can walk around it?

Think before you talk or act; it's hard to take back angry words. Better to be silent than to end up in trouble. If you're alert to other people's moods and problems, you'll find more people are willing to listen and help.

If you see it's a bad day for a friend, a teacher, or a parent, you might want to postpone making your request or talking about a problem. You'll get better advice or information when the other person has the time and energy to spend with you.

Or think: is there anybody else I can go to? Find an alternative to help you out.

When you care about someone who's not feeling so terrific, you could certainly offer your help, or tell a joke, or just join him or her for some companionship. Everyone needs a friendly ear now and then, or a pat on the back when life gets rough. It's normal. Handling your emotions all alone can be rough, so it's nice to know someone else cares.

Even if you can't change their situation, people really need to know that someone cares. Sometimes we hold all our problems inside because we don't want to bother anyone. That's the best part of having a close friend or a sympathetic parent. When you need to talk, they're close by to help.

As you talk with someone who's upset, remember that the person may listen but not follow your advice. What seems like a perfect solution to you might not be the best alternative for someone else. Your suggestions can be helpful if you respect the other person's right to choose his or her own course of action.

Try to consider other people's needs. You'll find that this works both ways. If you respect other people, they'll respect you. And this opens the door to worthwhile, open communication.

CHAPTER

three

BUILDING YOUR COMMUNICATION SKILLS

Did you ever know you were right but no one else believed you? It's not fair! you thought. Andy understands. It happened to him.

With two outs in the ninth inning, Andy caught a ground ball and quickly threw to first base. Although the umpire called the player safe, Andy knew he was really out and began to argue loudly with the umpire. Was this guy blind or what?

Coach Buckley called Andy in from the field.

"Why are you putting me on the bench, coach? What'd I do?" Andy asked angrily as he trotted in.

The coach looked at Andy seriously and said he understood his feelings. He'd also thought the runner was out, but players don't argue with the umpire.

Andy's face got hot and he struggled to hold back the stinging tears behind his eyes. It's not fair, he thought. I know I'm right. He crossed his arms and legs tightly and watched the team pack up.

The coach sat down and put his arm on Andy's shoulder.

"I'm sorry, Andy. If the umpire changed his decision each time a player yelled, the game would become a big shouting match!"

Andy was still angry. He couldn't meet the coach's eye. He looked down at the ground with a lump in his throat.

"We need you, Andy. You've got spirit and hustle. But when you act like a hothead, players lose control and concentration. And then they lose the game."

As he listened, Andy realized that the coach wasn't mad. His throat began to loosen up and he felt better inside. Even major league umpires make mistakes, he thought. Coach Buckley and Andy understood each other, communicating very well together.

LEARNING TO LISTEN

The key to better communication lies in good listening skills. Right now you're probably laughing and thinking: Even a baby knows how to listen!

Well, even if you can hear, that doesn't mean you listen well. Hearing is simple. Hearing involves recognizing sounds received by your ears.

Listening requires action. When you listen, you hear sounds. Then you use your intelligence to understand and link these sounds to your memory and thoughts.

Becoming a good listener can really improve your relationships.

When Tina's step-grandmother came to stay for a month, twelve-year-old Tina didn't even want to speak to her. She didn't know anything about the "old lady" and she didn't care.

Her father suggested she talk to Grandma Lucy

about women's clothing during World War II. So Tina asked her. She was intrigued to discover that Lucy had designed costumes for world-famous movie actresses during the 1940s and 1950s.

They watched some old movies together. Tina listened in surprise as Lucy described the fabrics, decorations, sizes, and prices of the beautiful dresses.

Grandma Lucy looked over Tina's clothes and helped her put together some very attractive outfits. And Tina's friends came over to meet her "famous" celebrity grandmother.

You can improve your listening skills. When you're ready to really listen, concentrate your thoughts on the speaker and ignore the other sounds around you.

Keep your eyes on the person speaking. This will help you listen better and will also tell the speaker that you're paying attention.

Want to know more about the speaker? Check her voice for clues. Not only what she says, but *how* she says it.

You may have noticed, for example, that many people speak much faster and have a higher pitched voice when they're nervous. Sometimes they say "uh" and "um" a lot. Shy people speak with lower, breathy voices.

Have you ever heard the president talk? Or the mayor? They use loud, deep voices, speaking slowly enough for everyone to understand. And their voices sound "important" and businesslike.

With a little practice, you can sound more like the people you admire.

How you use your voice can give words some very different meanings. Try this: Say the words "all done" as if you were in the following situations.

- Your leg cast was just removed after nine weeks;
- You've finished changing your bike's flat tire;
- Your father asks for a cupcake, and you ate the last one;
- You've written the last page of a long report;
- Your sister offers to help you *after* you've finished folding three loads of laundry;
- You've framed and hung your best painting.

Same words, different meanings. You've learned to use and understand many different speech patterns because people change their voices to fit the situation.

To remember most of what you hear, become an active listener. Review the most important points and ask yourself, do I need to know more? Then think about how you can use what you've learned.

An active listener remembers more information for a longer time than someone who barely pays attention. When you really listen, you learn more, you understand more, and you become a more interesting conversation partner.

You'll find that more people want to talk with you and enjoy spending time with you. Active listening actually helps both the speaker and the listener!

Practice your listening skills for a few days. Do you notice any changes in yourself? How has active listening affected your relationships?

HOLD BACK OR SPEAK OUT?

Early Tuesday morning, Bruce's first-period teacher told him that Mr. Wood, the principal, wanted to see him.

Bruce thought fast.

"What did I do wrong? Boy, am I in trouble! My dad will kill me!" By the time he got to Mr. Wood's office, Bruce was pretty upset.

"Someone's lying and blaming me. Mr. Wood should listen to my side first . . ." he thought. Nobody believes me, he decided, getting angrier and angrier.

Soon Mr. Wood came out. Bruce stood up with a tight throat and red face. He took a deep breath and started to defend himself, but Mr. Wood spoke quickly.

"Congratulations, Bruce. We've selected your drawing to go on the front of this year's graduation program."

What a surprise! Bruce let out his breath with relief. Nothing to worry about after all. Good thing he didn't start off the conversation with angry words!

Have you ever said something and immediately regretted your words? You're not alone. Many people find they speak before they think. It's a common communication problem.

Why is it a problem? As Bruce found out, sometimes you speak before you have enough information. Maybe you've misunderstood the situation or the other person's ideas. Worse, you might find you've arrived at the wrong conclusion. Your comments might turn out to be unwise, unwelcome, or unnecessary.

So when should you speak up and when should you hold back?

Many times a friend will call or come to see you to talk about a problem. Sometimes this friend might need your advice. On other occasions, a friend just wants to talk or needs to blow off some steam. Maybe he's just had a huge fight with his father, or she didn't make the basketball team. You can be a big help just by lending a friendly ear and being sympathetic. Silence works best in these situations. Your challenge: deciding how to respond.

Cara could tell by the way her mom slammed the door, the pots, and the refrigerator that she was in a bad mood. As she prepared dinner, Mom poured some wine. Cara's heart sank. She knew that her mother would probably end up passed out on the sofa soon, after some loud and upsetting yelling.

"Can I help you, Mom?" Cara asked hopefully. Sometimes she kept her mom company to prevent major trouble in the kitchen. After her mother suffered several bad cuts and burns working when she was drunk, Cara learned to watch carefully and volunteer for any cutting activities. She didn't enjoy this time together much, because her mother drank as she worked, and usually ended up picking on Cara. But Cara worried about her mother, and she tried to be cheerful, avoiding any arguments or problems.

This didn't always work for Cara, and she found it helpful to talk with the school guidance counselor about her problem. The counselor urged her to go to AlaTeen, the teenagers' self-help group for children of alcoholic parents. Up until then, Cara couldn't face anybody else with her secret. Lately, though, her mother got drunk more often and made her feel terrible. Should Cara speak up, or just try to go along? She had to think about it carefully.

You'll find there are times it's best not to answer back, comment, or give advice. Other times you may decide to voice your opinion, say what's on your mind, and join the discussion. You may not always make the right choice. Sometimes there's just *nothing* you can do to avoid a problem. Only you can make this decision.

Lots of people find silence uncomfortable. They try to speak quickly, filling the silence with anything that comes to mind. Silence sends its own messages.

What could silence mean? It depends on the setting, the people, the relationship. Sometimes silence means, "I'm so comfortable with you that we don't need to talk." On the other hand, there may be silence when two people don't know each other very well. They may be thinking of something to talk about.

Silence could also mean: I'm angry; I'm not interested; I'm too busy to think; I'm tired; I'd like some time alone; I'm frustrated; I need more information; I'm thinking about what you just said.

Sometimes what you *don't* say means a lot. Simon saw his little brother Jon take a cigarette from their father's pack. Simon tried to tell Jon that the cigarette would make him sick, but Jon insisted he could handle it.

Jon lit up down the block, aware that Simon was watching in the distance. Jon felt so grown up, holding the cigarette carefully between his fingers. He breathed in the smoke very slowly and deliberately; then he began to cough.

He immediately tried again, struggling to hold in his coughing and choking. Finally, Jon admitted defeat, throwing down the cigarette in disgust. He didn't come home right away, though. He was afraid his brother would make him feel worse by saying, "I told you so."

Simon didn't say a word. He could see that Jon felt bad enough already. Jon wouldn't be smoking again soon, he thought to himself.

So when should you speak and when should you keep silent? You have the opportunity to decide all the time.

You may find it helpful to take a moment to think. Consider how you will affect other people if you speak. Consider how they might react to you if you don't.

EXPRESSING YOURSELF CLEARLY

It takes two people to communicate: one to send the message and the other to receive it. You shouldn't be too surprised to discover that sometimes the other person doesn't receive the message you think you've sent.

In chapter two we discussed your emotions. Emotions may be expressed outwardly: crying, giggling, or frowning, for example. We understand these reactions most of the time.

Sometimes you may try to hide your emotions, try to ignore them or pretend they don't exist. Sometimes you don't want other people to know how you feel, or you wish you could change how you feel. Perhaps you're ashamed of feelings like jealousy or fright.

Most of the time you communicate a clear message. But sometimes you communicate a "mixed message" by saying something you don't believe in a way that confuses the other person.

Occasionally, you find yourself protecting people by hiding your true feelings. You may not be successful, however.

When Tracy visited her father, he tried out a new recipe for dinner. It turned out pretty bad. Tracy ate some without mentioning the taste. Her father noticed Tracy didn't eat with her usual speed. When he asked her about it, she pretended to like dinner.

She *said* she enjoyed the food, but her actions didn't match what she said. That's a mixed message.

Or perhaps you've sent a mixed message with your tone of voice. Remember the "all done" exercise? You use different tones to express different feelings, attitudes, and emotions.

Cheryl had a big fight with her best friend, Pat. When she got home from school, Cheryl called Pat to make up. Pat's mother told Cheryl that Pat wasn't home, but she'd call her back.

Cheryl waited two hours, then called again.

This time Pat anwered the phone. Cheryl invited her over to bake cookies, hoping to end the argument quickly. They usually enjoyed baking or cooking together. Pat told her she was sorry, she couldn't come.

"Why not?" Cheryl asked.

"My mom won't let me," Pat answered. "Maybe some other day." The words were right, but she sent a mixed message. Cheryl understood Pat's true feelings by her tone and quick refusal.

You probably understand some mixed messages very well. Scott sure did when his mom showed him a shirt she'd bought for his father. Scott thought the shirt looked too wild for his father, but he didn't want to say so. He was afraid to hurt her feelings.

"Great shirt, isn't it?" Mom asked, admiring the shirt.

Although she asked for Scott's opinion, do you think she really wanted to hear what he thought? Were they both giving a mixed message?

Other mixed messages may be harder to ac-

... BUT I ORDERED A BUNCH OF CARROTS !

cept. When Deirdre's father punished her for coming home too late, she felt hurt. Why didn't her father trust her?

They got into an argument over her curfew, and Deirdre screamed that her father didn't love her. If he loved her, she yelled, he wouldn't punish her! Her father yelled back, "Of course, I love you! I love you a lot! That's why I'm punishing you!"

At that point, Deirdre couldn't believe her father's mixed message: anger and punishment equals love. Can you explain that?

You don't always intend to send mixed messages. Sometimes you're busy or tired, or have a lot on your mind. Strong emotions can also affect your communication.

Some people cry when they're very happy; some people giggle when they're frightened, uncomfortable, or nervous. These powerful feelings sometimes show up unexpectedly. It's hard to keep them under control. Have you ever felt this way?

SAY WHAT YOU MEAN

No matter what message you send, it's best if you make clear exactly what's on your mind.

"I'm leaving," Kathy called from the front door.

"Where to?" asked her stepfather Jerry.

"Did you forget? The sleepover party at Sherri's house," Kathy answered. "Gotta go. I'll call tomorrow morning."

Jerry looked upset. "Tonight your mom and I are going out to dinner with my boss. We're counting on you to babysit Christian. In fact, we have to leave in an hour."

"But I told you about this party last week. Don't you remember?" Kathy was mad. As usual, no one had listened to her.

"You said Sherri had to check with her mother about the party," Jerry said. "It wasn't really definite. Anyway, yesterday I mentioned that my boss invited us to dinner. . . . I guess I didn't say when, did I?"

Both Jerry and Kathy tried to communicate. Each person sent a simple message. And each believed that the other person understood what they meant. Neither of them felt it was necessary to explain or talk further. As it turned out, neither one had a clear idea of the other's message. What happened?

Many of us make this mistake and assume that other people understand what we mean. We believe that our thoughts are so obvious that practically anyone will understand.

But as Kathy and Jerry found out, you must explain yourself to communicate. You can't assume that others can read your mind.

Peggy looked forward to visiting her father every other weekend. But she didn't enjoy the speech her mother made to her every time she packed up to go.

"Tell your father I'd appreciate his checks on time, please. He's three weeks behind now. I can't pay the bills and buy your clothes without his money. He's a real cheapskate, anyway. Never spent a penny without a fight. . . ." Her mother usually went on like this, complaining and criticizing. Peggy's stomach tightened into a knot.

She hated to talk to her father about money. She didn't want him to think she was only interested in the money. She really needed to spend some quiet time with him, alone. Asking about child support payments soured his mood quickly. He said she sounded just like her mother.

Peggy finally decided she couldn't stand feeling so trapped. She told her mother she couldn't ask about the check anymore because it made her feel bad inside. Then she asked if her mother knew what she meant. Her mother looked startled for a moment.

"I'm only looking out for your welfare, Peggy," her mother told her. "We need that money very badly, you know."

"I'll feel much better if you and Dad work it out without my help, Mom," Peggy said in a choked whisper.

"If you feel that way, I'll call him. You know I hate to talk with him, but I'll do it for you."

Peggy just assumed her mother knew how much she dreaded asking about money. She'd never really discussed the issue. How do you think Peggy could have avoided this conflict?

Say what you mean. Make sure your message is received and understood. To make sure it is heard, ask for a response.

Suppose you're planning to meet a friend at 2:00 and need a ride from your mother. Ask your mom if 2:00 is convenient.

If you've spent half an hour explaining to your parents why you're upset with your younger sister or brother, ask them if they understand your problem. You might want some suggestions or ideas to help you cope.

BODY LANGUAGE

Yes, your body talks! In fact, years of research show that more feelings are communicated by your face and body than by the words you say.

Even when you try to hide your feelings, someone who understands *body language* will know your true feelings. Your words may say one thing, but your body may communicate something totally different.

That's how Mom knows you're the one who broke the glass or spilled grape juice on the rug. She knows you well enough to see the truth "on your face" even when you say, "I didn't do it."

You can learn to understand body language, too. Professionals have studied how Americans move. Here is just a sampling that may interest you.

USES OF BODY LANGUAGE

If You Do This . . .	*It Usually Means*
Lean toward the person	You like or you're interested in the person you're with
Stand far away	You don't like or don't trust that person
Cross arms in conversation	You're uncomfortable or not interested
Tap toes, pick at nails	You're not listening or are impatient
Don't look someone in the eyes	You're keeping a secret, not telling the truth, or very shy

Next time you're in the cafeteria, the gym, or a store, look at the people around you. Observe their body language as they talk. Do you recognize any of these movements? What do they mean?

You have become used to the body language that you see around you every day. But these movements might mean something totally different to people in another country. Every culture develops its own gestures and meanings.

Body language includes the expressions on your face, your posture, how you hold your body. Everybody has his or her own special way of standing, sitting, walking, and leaning. And each movement helps you show how you feel.

Ask a good friend to check up on you during a school day. Can he or she read your face and body to find out how you feel? Do you express your feelings the way you want to?

Some people get into the habit of using certain expressions and movements over and over. We call these movements mannerisms. Do you have a friend who says "you know" in every sentence? Do you know someone who clears her throat every few seconds?

Mannerisms develop slowly over time. They help some people control their nervous energy. When you're tense or tired, you might find yourself using a familiar mannerism. Common mannerisms include tapping a pen or pencil, licking lips, twirling hair, saying "like" or "OK" all the time.

If you have a mannerism you'd like to stop using, experts say you can do it. Begin by noticing. Then take a deep breath, slow down, and change. Find out how often you do it, and in what situations. Are you nervous at this time? Or has your mannerism simply become a habit that you practice all the time? A friend can help. Ask your friend to hold up a hand every time you say "you know." You'll become more aware of your speech this way.

According to the researchers, you'll find it easier to substitute something new. Each time you find yourself beginning the mannerism, *stop* and try another, smaller movement. You might try crossing your fingers or rubbing your toes, for instance. After a while, you'll find you've replaced the old mannerism with something new that hardly shows.

Good communication between people helps reduce stress and improves relationships. You'll be more relaxed and easier to be with. Better communication skills work well with your friends, your family, teachers, and coaches. You'll use these skills in everyday activities like dating, shopping, and working.

And as you mature and gain more self-confidence, you'll find it easier to communicate successfully. This will help you understand yourself and other people better, and they will understand and respect you.

CHAPTER

UNDERSTANDING
THE ADULTS
IN YOUR LIFE

You probably know a lot about your parents and close relatives by now. Over time you learn about each of your school teachers, your music instructor, scout leader, team coach, family doctor, and the librarian.

As we discussed in chapter one, these people have many roles. You may know them in their professional life, their personal life, or both. They have a job to do or a service to perform. This is a responsibility that most adults take seriously and work hard to complete.

Just as your family members share your life, these other people are part of your life also, some more than others. And we're all part of a community, where members live and work together.

YOU AND YOUR FAMILY

Your family is unique, because no other family has *you!* Small or large, each family unit works in its own way.

Joe's family has six children. Because his mother works, he's expected to watch his younger sister and brothers. When the children want something, they go to Joe for help. Joe finds himself answering a lot of questions, fixing snacks, washing off dirty scratches, and soothing hurt feelings.

Other families may have only one or two children. Some families have one parent living one place and the other someplace else. Children may stay with one parent during school months and visit the other on weekends, vacations, and holidays. These young people actually belong to two family units, each with its own way of operating.

Barbara's parents were divorced two years ago. She spends two weekends a month with her father and calls him during the week just to say "hi" and talk. When she visits her dad, they usually go out for pizza or hamburgers. On Sunday she enjoys making pancakes or waffles just for the two of them. They look for an old movie on television and watch it while they snack together.

At her mother's house, Barbara eats cereal or toast for a quick Sunday breakfast. She listens to the radio while her mother reads the Sunday papers. Then they work together, changing the bedsheets and folding laundry.

What is your family like? You've been a member of your family for a long time. Do you know what your father likes to do when he's relaxing? Do you know your mother's favorite food? What kind of music does your sister or brother enjoy?

Your family knows you too. They know your favorite TV programs and your friends. They're used to your sense of humor and they know what bothers you.

Maybe you've changed your style of dressing lately. You're listening to different music, or you don't eat carrots anymore. Your parents ask a lot of questions about your new ideas and you're tired of explaining. You think that no one undertands you.

You're growing and changing so fast that they might not be able to keep up with you! It takes time for your family to adjust to the new you in progress.

WHAT DO PARENTS EXPECT?

Parents were not born old. Just like you, they began their lives as babies and grew to childhood and adolescence. They became adults in the same way you will, by trying new ideas, making mistakes, and working on new skills. Just like you, at times they succeeded and at times they failed.

Your mother and father learned some important lessons as they grew up. They learned about people and how to tell right from wrong. They developed a system of *values*, deep beliefs to guide their lives. These values are based on their family background and their religion, schooling, and life experiences.

As adults, your parents live according to their values. You've probably noticed that they don't always agree on everything. Because they grew up in different families and with different experiences, their values may not be alike. This can cause conflict.

Most parents try to agree on important things to teach their children. They try to discuss ideas together and make decisions about how to raise their family.

This is a very difficult part of being a parent

because it affects the lives of the whole family. Because they feel their values are important, parents work hard to make sure their children understand and follow them.

Your parents may want you to be honest, helpful, clean, studious, punctual, or hardworking. Or they may have other values that they want you to accept.

How do parents help their children learn values? A lot of parents tell their children how to behave.

"No whining!" "Say please." "Don't talk back to Grandma." Your parents send you messages so you'll know what they want. As you read in chapter three, these messages could be easy to understand, or you might have to think a little. Sometimes you're not sure.

When your parents say "be careful," do you know what they mean? Are they warning you to cross the street carefully? Spend your money wisely? Eat properly?

Maybe they'll look at you a certain way. Sometimes you'll get a "look" that says "don't do that again." Or a motion of your mother's hand might tell you, "let's talk about that later."

The longer you live with your parents, the better you understand their body language and the special tones of their voices.

So what do parents expect from their children? That's a hard question. Most parents have some idea of how they'd like their child to grow up. These expectations could include college, career, hobbies and interests, even marriage and children.

Twelve-year-old Peter is getting tired of hearing his parents talk about how they can't wait for

Peter to graduate from high school and join the army. His older brother enlisted two years ago. His father and his grandfather spent their entire careers in the military too.

Peter's parents keep pushing him toward the army because, they tell him, he needs to grow up.

"You'll become a man!" his father says all the time. And his mother chimes in, telling him what a great opportunity it is to get an education and learn a trade.

Peter's upset because he has no interest in military life. For the last two years he's spent all his free time at the computer, writing programs and trying out new ideas. Peter wants to go to college to work with computers. The army is the last place he sees himself.

He's tried to talk to his parents about his feelings, but every time he brings up the subject, they tell him not to worry. His parents believe he'll change his mind when he's older. They don't take his feelings seriously. Peter's angry and a little worried about the future.

Peter has decided to ask his older brother for advice. He thinks that his brother will understand his feelings. He also hopes his brother will help him discuss the problem with their parents.

On the other hand, eleven-year-old Lindsay finds her parents pushing her to go to college. They want her to be a teacher or a nurse. They tell her these jobs will be the easiest for her to manage when Lindsay becomes a mother.

Lindsay doesn't know if she wants to get married or have children. She wants to stay after school on Mondays and Wednesdays for dance club because she secretly hopes to become a professional dancer.

After dinner one night, Lindsay asked her mom for a serious talk. She quietly explained her love for dancing and her hope for a dance career. If she didn't have to babysit her younger brother Tom, she said, she could join the dance club.

Her mother didn't think Lindsay was realistic about her chance to become a dancer. Dancers don't make much money, she told Lindsay. Besides, it would be hard for her to pay someone to babysit Tom.

They discussed many different ideas. Lindsay called her friend Lisa, who took care of her own brother after school. Lisa offered to babysit on Wednesdays if Lindsay would help her on another day. After a while, Lindsay's mother said that Lindsay could join the dance club. She would pay a neighbor to watch Tom on Mondays. They also agreed to ask the instructor about Lindsay's talent and the chances for a real dance career.

Young people often face these situations with their parents. It's not always easy for you to understand your parents' point of view, and they don't always understand yours, either. This can cause problems, arguments, and hurt feelings.

PARENTS ARE PEOPLE

Do you ever think you have your parents figured out, and then they surprise you by doing something you don't expect?

For almost a year, Harriet had been asking her mother to let her go out after dark. She wanted to join her friends standing around the corner deli. It was only one block away, and not dark at all, she said. And she'd come home right on time, promise.

One day Harriet came home from school and found a note on the kitchen table. "Go ahead and get gorgeous—you can go out tonight. Call me later. Love, Mom." Harriet couldn't believe her eyes! At last, permission to go out after dark. Why do you think Harriet's parent changed her mind?

Mature adults usually think over the decisions they make. They try to be fair and use facts to make up their minds.

But because parents are human too, they don't always have logical reasons for the things they do. The events of the day, their mood, or personal problems could affect the decisions they make.

Worried parents may not display their usual patience or understanding. Caring for a sick child or relative, marital difficulties, job problems, money worries, and other important difficulties sometimes make it hard for adults to pay attention to their children. They could be short-tempered, yell, or bang the dishes. Or they might send you to bed early so they can talk.

How do you react when your parents are under stress? Some young people use this time to do things without permission. Their parents are too busy to check up on them, so they're not afraid of getting caught.

Roy began to skip school after his father entered a drug-treatment program in the city. None of his friends knew where his father had gone, but Roy felt alone and angry. His mother cried a lot at night. She didn't pay much attention to Roy's homework or school needs, and he wasn't in the mood to ask for help, either. So he wandered around, looking for things to do.

Sometimes he'd take money from his mother's purse and go to the movies. Other times he'd go to a busy store and shoplift small items, thinking how smart he was. He no longer felt comfortable with his old friends, because he had to protect his dad's painful secret. What a terrible time for Roy.

Other young people try to behave unusually well, hoping this will help their parents through the stressful period. They may push themselves further than usual, seeking perfection as a reaction to their problems at home. In some families the children continue their everyday activities.

If your parent has a serious problem with alcohol or drug abuse, you know it can be hard to live with a person who is unpredictable. Or perhaps one of your parents faces major surgery or is struggling with a medical emergency. These situations challenge everyone's ability to act maturely.

Every day presents a fresh opportunity for you to change your behavior. You're always trying new ways to cope with your family's problems.

THINKING ABOUT DIVORCE AND STEPFAMILIES

When your parents get divorced, you have to get used to an entirely new life. One parent usually moves to a new home.

Your parents may not agree on many things. They might not talk to each other at all, or they might yell a lot. You need a lot of patience to keep smiling through the first year of their divorce.

Then, when you've finally got everything under control, you find one of your parents is getting married. You've got a stepparent.

Who is this new family member? Your father or mother loves this person. They've chosen to share their lives together. And *you* are part of the package.

You may not be happy about this new situation. Even though your stepparent tries to be friendly, it's hard to adjust to another adult in your family.

Laurie's parents were divorced three years ago. Her father, Frank, introduced his friend, Ann, last year, and now they're getting married. Laurie has been thinking about it, and she's very unhappy.

Before her father met Ann, their visits were such fun! Laurie would pick out some place to visit and he always agreed. But when Ann and Frank became engaged, he began to ask Ann to join them on some weekend visits. They held hands and kissed. If Ann didn't feel like riding bikes, they didn't go. And they never went to any Mexican restaurants anymore, because Ann didn't like Mexican food.

Laurie pointed out Ann's faults to her mother. She knew her mother was upset about the new marriage. Her mother listened and told Laurie that she understood her feelings. Laurie was angry, hurt, and a little jealous of Ann.

They discussed these emotions and talked about Laurie's fears. She was afraid her father would move far away. She didn't want her father to have another baby and forget about her. She was worried that Ann would boss her around. Laurie's mom suggested that Laurie try to talk with her father privately about her feelings.

So Laurie picked a quiet moment and told her father about her fears. To her surprise, he understood her feelings. They talked about Ann, marriage, and children.

After they had this discussion, Laurie began to relax a little. She wasn't really happy about the changes, but she became used to the idea of her father's marriage. As the date approached, she promised her father that she'd try to get along with

Ann. Her father made a special effort to spend more time alone with Laurie.

Laurie was lucky because her mother and father helped her accept her new stepmother. By practicing her communication skills, Laurie began to build her relationship with Ann.

Stepparents are people, too. They have emotions, needs, and plans for the future. They express their thoughts and values to their partner (your parent.) As in any relationship, you should expect some differences of opinion. And you may not enjoy the company, at first.

It may feel strange in the beginning to wake up with different people around you. But you can begin to build a relationship with your stepparent. He or she will be a part of your life for a long time. This new role means more responsibility for the stepparent, also. If your stepparent has a child or several children, you'll have to adjust to them as well.

Your parent and new stepparent may have children together, a half-sister or half-brother for you. You'll probably be a little anxious and jealous with a new baby getting so much attention.

Forming new families isn't easy. You'll be living with new personalities and meeting new relatives too. Both families will share holidays, vacations, and other free time during the year.

Building these relationships takes time and patience for you as well as for your stepparent. You'll both benefit from the experience.

GETTING ALONG WITH TEACHERS AND STAFF

Of course, your family isn't the only group you belong to. You're part of a school community too.

You spend a lot of time at school, involved with lessons, learning, and other activities.

You may be working with your classroom teacher, other subject teachers, librarian, coaches, the school nurse, secretary, principal, guidance counselor, or reading specialist.

The school staff works with students, parents, and community members to make your school a place for learning. All the members of the school "family" work together to make the building a good, safe place for everyone.

How do you fit in? You're an important member of the school society on several levels. As a student, you work with books, computers, films, and other materials. You're busy discovering facts and forming attitudes about the world around you. And you contribute to your school by helping to keep your classroom, lunchroom, gym, and desk clean.

You carry on relationships with many members of the school society. You have friends in your class and in other classes. You may be a monitor who helps a teacher or other staff member. Perhaps you've joined a school club or team. You have quite a variety of roles in your school.

You probably know that school staffers have different personalities and communication styles. They deal with you as an individual, and you have to deal with each one of them in an individual way too.

What do teachers want from you? Teachers are professionals, but they are also people. They work toward many goals during the school day.

Mrs. Shea, for instance, teaches sixth grade social studies. She's been working on a new unit about South America. She's gathered pictures and articles about South American farmland, occupations, languages, climate, and population. In addition, she selected a dozen library books and a film.

Mrs. Shea is worried that she won't have enough time to finish this exciting unit. It's close to the end of the school year, and her class is preparing for graduation. One of her students broke her arm, and the class is making her a special card and present.

Mrs. Shea also has to clean the room, empty the bookshelves, and pack up the posters and artwork for next year. There's a Parent-Teacher meeting tomorrow, and she's trying to find a babysitter to watch her six-year-old son. And she's planning to visit her brother in the hospital this weekend. Mrs. Shea has a lot on her mind.

Just like parents, teachers don't always have patience and understanding in the classroom. They are also busy with events, activities, and problems.

Don't expect to have trouble with your teachers. Try to be aware of their personalities and styles of communication. Then you'll be able to work with each one in a suitable way.

Are you thinking, "Why should *I* have to be the one to pay attention to these details? Why can't my (teacher, principal, coach, etc.) be more careful in communications with *me?* That's their job!"

Think of all the students these people deal with each day. They may see a hundred or more on some days. And they also have to work with the principal, the school board, and parents in the community. School staffers try hard to get to know as many students as they can, but sometimes they're just too busy.

As you probably know by now, life isn't fair. In

an ideal world, you'd have only enthusiastic, terrific teachers who know you and your abilities. But in the real world, you should expect to come across a teacher who's having a bad day, or who has a lot on his or her mind. In fact, you may find a teacher who just doesn't like you. This happens occasionally, and it's a very difficult situation.

Elinor had a painful experience last fall with her science teacher. Elinor usually knew all the answers, so Mrs. Black never called on her to answer the more basic questions. The few times Elinor didn't raise her hand, Mrs. Black chose her to answer the hardest questions. Elinor tried her best, but she was very embarrassed. No one in the class understood why Mrs. Black treated her this way.

Elinor felt terrible. She wouldn't talk to her parents about it because she didn't want to be a crybaby. Elinor's mother noticed that she never talked about science class anymore. She sat down with Elinor for a quiet talk. Elinor began to cry and told her mother how she felt.

Elinor's mother made an appointment with the school guidance counselor, and they decided to set up a meeting. Mrs. Black, the guidance counselor, and Elinor's mother got together the next afternoon.

Elinor's mother explained how Elinor felt. Mrs. Black listened and then explained that she knew what a great science student Elinor was. She felt she should give other students a chance to answer the easier questions. She wanted to challenge Elinor with more difficult work.

Mrs. Black said she didn't realize how this hurt Elinor's feelings, and she was sorry. She promised to call on Elinor more often.

ADULTS AT WORK

You come into contact with many different adults during the course of the year. Many of them will be "on duty" when you're with them. On most days you see police officers patrolling the streets. You may hear the fire engines as firefighters rush to a fire.

If your family worships in a church or synagogue, you'll see the minister, priest, rabbi, or other important religious leaders. You visit your dentist and your doctor for checkups.

You usually see these people in their professional roles. They use their experience and knowledge to offer you guidance and advice. Of course, that doesn't mean that you will always follow their suggestions. However, you may use their help in gathering information about and identifying alternatives to various situations.

These people have important responsibilities and authority. They're used to being in charge of most situations. And most believe that they know quite a lot about their specialty.

Some of these adults may offer you advice without being asked. You may not want to listen to what they're saying. You may not agree with what they tell you. And they may not agree with what you do or say to them.

Good communication can help when you deal with these adults in authority. Sharpen your listening and observation skills so you can hold up your end of the conversation. Ask questions and explain and discuss the issues as calmly as possible.

These extra efforts may prevent unnecessary problems, although you shouldn't expect all adults to be mature and reasonable. There are some adults, as well as some young people, who use any excuse to display bad temper and behave in an inconsiderate manner.

EXPECT SOME CONFLICT

At this point in your life, you've gained many skills. In fact, you can take care of yourself pretty well. You know right from wrong, and you've become quite efficient at many everyday activities.

But you're still too young for some privileges, like driving a car or traveling overnight alone with your friends. And your parents may not think you're ready to assume some responsibilities like shopping for your own shoes and clothes, or setting your own curfew.

While you may be eager to make your own life decisions, your parents may not feel you're ready. And this difference of opinion leads to conflict.

As you grow and mature, you'll find yourself questioning your parents' judgment. Sometimes you'll think your parents are wrong. Later on you may discover they were right. Or you might discover that they were wrong. On other occasions, you may agree with them, but you don't want to give in because you want to get your own way. So you discuss what's on your mind.

How you express yourself is almost as important as the subject you're discussing. The adults will be evaluating your behavior as they evaluate your request. They usually measure your maturity by how you act.

Greg learned his lesson the hard way. His friends asked him to go to a hot new movie, rated "R." Greg's parents didn't allow him to see "R"

HE'S MAD BECAUSE HE SAYS WE TREAT HIM LIKE A CHILD !
BANG!
THUMP
THUMP
THUMP
CRASH!
THUMP!
SMASH!!

movies because they didn't approve of all the sex and violence for a thirteen-year-old. So Greg didn't tell them exactly where he was going, and he set out for the movie theater.

The cashier wouldn't sell the group tickets because they looked much younger than seventeen. Greg's friends began to ask the adults in line to buy tickets for them and escort them into the theater. When no one would help, the boys started to curse and shout at the adults. Since the boys couldn't get into the movies, they bought ice cream and later went home.

Greg arrived home to find his parents upset. One boy's parents had called to tell about the boys' behavior at the movies. How did they know? A neighbor was on line waiting to get in.

Although his parents asked him to explain, Greg began to shout, "You never let me do anything! You treat me like a baby! I can't wait till I'm eighteen 'cause I'm moving out." His father grounded him for a month and sent him to bed.

When his parents discussed the matter later, they agreed that Greg didn't act in a very mature way. His behavior proved to them that they were right to restrict his privileges. Do you think they will change their minds soon? What could Greg do that might cause his parents to reconsider?

Many young people challenge authority. It's a normal part of growing up. If your requests concern minor issues, there's a good chance the adults will give in if you have good reasons to offer them.

As you get older, this may not satisfy you. You'll be exploring the world, looking for new experiences and information. You may feel that you want to try different activities that your parents may not have allowed when you were younger.

You'll probably find it harder to get permission for some of these projects. On the other hand, your parents' answers might surprise you.

All the adults you know traveled this same road to self-identity. It's a tough journey. They've had their ups and downs, their troubles and their fun. Just like you, they learned from their experiences, growing and maturing into adulthood.

CHAPTER

COMPROMISE
OR CONFRONTATION?

"Today is the first day of the rest of your life." You may have heard this expression before. Many old sayings express important messages. And this one is particularly true for people like you who are preparing for your future.

You've had a lot of experience dealing with adults. Some of these occasions have been positive and some have been negative. Now you're ready to make some adjustments for the challenges still ahead of you.

BEING HONEST

One of your most difficult tasks may appear quite simple: learning to be honest with yourself. What's so hard about this? It requires courage to analyze your thoughts and actions. You need to look at yourself from time to time and think about what you've said and done.

One afternoon Daniel walked home with Justin, as usual. They passed the same apartment house each day. It was boarded up after a fire last year. As they approached the building this time, however, Justin looked at Daniel with a sparkle in his eye.

"Want to see something amazing?" asked Justin, heading toward the back of the building.

They put down their books, and Justin reached deep into his jeans pocket, pulling out a marijuana cigarette.

"I bought this joint off Eddie yesterday. He says it's the best around. We'll get real high!" Justin grinned.

Daniel helped Justin light up, his head brimming with thoughts. On the one hand, Daniel was rather curious. He had never even seen marijuana, and now he had an opportunity to smoke some. But deep in his heart, he was also a little afraid. He remembered what his parents and teachers had said about drugs. There were many dangers and problems.

Leaning against the building, Daniel began to feel dizzy. He didn't want Justin to think he was "chicken" if he didn't smoke marijuana. He also wasn't ready to be pressured into smoking. He needed time to think. So he took a deep breath and turned to Justin.

"I just remembered—my book report is due tomorrow. If I smoke this stuff, I won't be able to read or write too well. We'd better hurry home to hit the books." Daniel reached down, picked up Justin's books, and held them out. Justin looked at him for a moment, slightly embarrassed. Then he put out the marijuana cigarette.

"Maybe tomorrow, huh?" Justin asked. Daniel didn't answer. He had the feeling that Justin wasn't too sure about this stuff, either. Daniel intended to think seriously about the incident, and decide what he could do in the future. Do you have any ideas about what Daniel could do to change the situation?

If you're using the decision-making model, you probably have several suggestions for Daniel. He could tell Justin that he's not interested in drugs; he could avoid the topic whenever it comes up; he could grab the joint and throw it away. You may have other good ideas he could use.

But Daniel has already taken the most important step: he's learned to be honest with himself. He's decided that he needs more time to study his response, and he's thinking about his next move.

You probably know that it can be hard to apologize. Some people don't know when they're wrong; others hate to admit it. And some people turn things around and blame others for their errors. Do you know people who do this? How does it make you feel?

Even if you can't admit a mistake or flaw to anyone else, it's important to be honest with yourself. That can be tough because no one likes to be wrong. It feels a lot better to be right.

People often pretend to themselves. Sometimes you may want to convince yourself that you're quite good at a certain task or skill, even if you're not. You like to feel important and special.

Or perhaps you want other people to think you're better at something than you really are. Then you puff out your chest, talk like you're terrific, and "bluff" your way through.

It's usually easier to fool other people than to fool yourself, you'll find. Deep down, you know the truth. It's important to admit the truth to yourself, and know the difference between real life and wishful thinking.

If you've said or done something you regret, you should be able to apologize. But when you find yourself doing plenty of apologizing, this is probably a signal that it's time to make some changes in your life.

You can begin by analyzing your behavior. You may find it hard at first to think about yourself and what you've done. If you can learn from these episodes, you'll be able to make changes in your future behavior on your way to adulthood.

OPEN YOURSELF UP
TO NEW IDEAS

Wouldn't it be great if you never made a mistake, never lost your temper, never gave up in the middle of a task? While you may achieve these goals on some occasions, it's impossible to reach all of your goals all of the time.

No matter how perfect someone may appear on the surface, he or she certainly has some feature that could be worked on. You might have heard about "building character." Successful people do this all the time. It's an important part of growing up. It means using all of your experiences, the good ones as well as the painful ones, to help you change yourself into the person you want to be.

As you grow, you learn that the most interesting, best-liked, and successful people around you are constantly learning, changing, and experimenting with new ideas about themselves and their lives. They view each day as a chance to try something a little different or enjoy a new experience.

This doesn't have to mean "wild" or "crazy." It could be something that you've never done. Or working at your ordinary activities in a different way. Perhaps you'll try pitching instead of playing first base, reading a book about someone you've never heard of, or volunteering to wash the dishes without being asked. New behaviors, new thoughts, new places, new foods, and new friends—all milestones on the path of life.

Each day you can allow yourself the freedom to explore positive new ways of thinking and to make some changes. You don't have to let difficulties in your past control your future.

Wendy recently discovered this. She's always found social studies dull and boring. Wendy didn't pay much attention in class, and she hated to read the textbook. She barely passed social studies in elementary school.

When Wendy got to seventh grade, she was prepared to sleep through social studies again. She didn't even open the textbook in September. In October the teacher assigned group projects. Wendy and three other students had to research and tell the class about politics during the American Civil War.

Because her work affected the entire project, the other students wouldn't let Wendy do a sloppy job. They helped her use the library card catalogue, select books, and prepare a clear outline for the presentation. Little by little, as she worked, Wendy found herself reading more about the Civil War. She became curious about the battles, the weapons, and the soldiers' lives.

By the end of November, her social studies grade had improved. Her test marks rarely dipped below B, and she raised her hand in class every day.

Wendy thought about this change. She realized that just because she had been bored with social studies in elementary school, she didn't have to always be bored. The committee project opened her mind to an exciting new area of social studies. She allowed herself to enjoy the assignment and learn something, too.

This experience changed Wendy's attitude toward social studies. She began to look forward to the challenge of new ideas. And she gained confidence in her ability to learn. Wendy took a negative experience and turned it into a positive one.

You'll find, just as Wendy did, that a problem in the past doesn't have to mean a problem in the present. You can master all kinds of skills if your mind is open and you keep trying to learn.

OPINIONS OR FACTS?

Many adults are concerned about you and the things you say and do. Your work is evaluated at school, your achievements and behavior are examined at home, your skills and performance are monitored by your coach, club, or scout leader. It sometimes feels like all these people spend their time telling you what to do and how to do it.

In a way, you may be right. As we discussed in chapter four, these adults have expectations for you. Each of them, in a unique way, has some interest in your decisions, your life, or your education. They may tell you what they think, whether you ask for their opinion or not. And if you think about it, you probably offer your opinions to people who may or may not be interested in them.

So it's important to understand the difference between an opinion and a fact. Your opinion is simply a statement of what you believe. That doesn't make it right or wrong, true or false. Opinions are ideas and thoughts that could be correct or incorrect.

For instance, you may see a painting in a museum and say to your friend, "That's ugly!" You're giving your opinion. Your friend may agree or disagree, depending on what he or she thinks about the painting.

Facts, however, are very different. Facts are always true. Facts describe real situations, events, and things that cannot be changed. Suppose you turned to your friend in the museum and said, "That painting is full of dark blue triangles." Now you're stating a fact about the painting. Anyone who wants to check this fact can look at the painting to see the triangles.

There are many ways to learn whether something is true. You can look in an encyclopedia, book, newspaper, or almanac. You can ask someone else who might know. Or you can look for evidence that shows what happened.

When you offer an opinion, remember that what you say may only be true for you. You may not want to go to the beach on Saturday because you find it boring. However, your father, mother, and sister look forward to swimming, reading, and building sand castles. They're not bored at the beach. Your family may decide to go to the beach even though you don't enjoy it. This doesn't make them right or wrong. It's just a matter of different opinions.

On the other hand, some opinions may be true for a large number of people. Suppose your neighbor begins to blast his stereo very late one night. Your father might bang on the wall or call on the phone and tell him that the music is too loud. He'd ask the neighbor to turn the sound down. How loud is "loud"? That is a matter of opinion. But if many people find themselves awakened by this music, then it must be too loud.

Some people may not agree with your opinion.

Others might think you're 100 percent correct. In either case, it helps to remember that an opinion isn't the same as a fact. Be prepared for some discussion, but respect other people's opinions.

When you disagree with someone, that doesn't automatically make them wrong. They simply see things differently than you do. If you want people to respect your opinions, stay calm. Present any facts that support your position. Try to explain yourself clearly. Or use an example that will help other people understand your thoughts and ideas.

Many discussions end with people still on opposite sides of the same question. If you conduct yourself with dignity and maturity, you'll find that people will admire you for your style.

FOCUS ON YOURSELF WITHOUT ATTACKING OTHERS

Jordan was excited to be chosen for a big part in the school play. The entire cast worked hard for months to memorize their lines. Two weeks before the show was scheduled to open, the director, Mr. Tilman, decided to make some last-minute changes. He changed some of the talking parts and moved around two scenes.

But Jordan and the other students didn't have enough time to practice the new scenes. A week before the play, the actors only knew half the lines. They didn't even know when to enter or leave the stage.

Jordan asked his mother for advice. His mother told him that he should talk to Mr. Tilman and tell him how the changes were upsetting the cast. But his mother also reminded him that no one likes to be criticized. So she suggested that Jordan choose his words carefully. Instead of attacking Mr. Tilman, she told Jordan to focus on personal feelings.

Jordan went to see Mr. Tilman at lunchtime the next day.

"I'm really nervous, Mr. Tilman," Jordan started out. "Last week I had the play memorized so well that I could say my lines in my sleep. But I'm finding it difficult to learn more lines, and I'm having trouble working with the new scenes.

"We open next week," Jordan continued, "and I'm scared it's going to be a flop. We were so good before the changes, can't we go back to the original play?" Jordan found it hard to say this without showing how upset he was. But he knew that he would have a better chance to persuade Mr. Tilman to change his mind if he wasn't too pushy.

Jordan could see that Mr. Tilman was very surprised.

"Do you think a lot of the actors feel this way?" Mr. Tilman asked. Jordan nodded. "Then I guess we'd better talk about this at today's rehearsal. Maybe we can agree on what to do about the play. I'm glad you came to see me, Jordan."

Jordan expressed his opinion, but he was careful not to attack Mr. Tilman. He spoke about his own feelings and his ideas. He didn't call names or criticize Mr. Tilman's work.

You'll find that many mature adults will listen when you focus on explaining your own feelings. Suppose you want to stay out a little later with your friends, but your father won't let you. You could tell your father, "You treat me like a baby. You never let me do anything!" Or you could say, "I'm more responsible now that I'm older. I'd like the chance to show you that I'm ready for a later curfew." Which approach might be more likely to persuade your father?

If you begin to yell, accuse, or criticize the adults, you may find that they "tune you out." Or they'll dismiss your request as immature. But if you try to present your opinion in terms of "I-statements," you'll find it easier to make these people understand your needs.

There may be times when an adult won't let you explain how you feel. You may not be able to say a word. This will probably make you angry and frustrated. And you may find it difficult to hold your temper. When you act maturely, you can be proud of your behavior and self control.

TRY SUGGESTIONS
INSTEAD OF CRITICISM

As you've learned from your own experiences, most people find it painful to be criticized, even when they know that the criticism is true. As we discussed earlier, it can be very hard to look at yourself honestly.

There are some adults who find it difficult to accept criticism from a younger person. Just like you, adults prefer to think of themselves as competent. Criticism can be just as painful for an adult.

If there's something you want to tell one of the adults in your life, you'll have the best chance for success if you avoid criticizing. Try to turn your criticism into a suggestion.

Megan tried this method with her grandparents recently. She usually stays with her grandparents during winter vacation. They have always told her that they're afraid she'll get hurt or have an accident when she's at their house. So they won't let her see any of her friends, go to the movies, bowl, or even go to the store alone. Megan tried to get her grandparents to change their minds for the past two years, but she's had no luck.

This year, instead of talking about how over-protective they are, she began to discuss their fears with them. They talked about safety, the dangers of strangers, and gangs. Megan listened and tried to understand their feelings.

Then Megan suggested some ways she could safely enjoy herself. She suggested a small get-to-gether at her grandparents' apartment, so they could meet her friends. She asked about another friend's parent going to the store or movies with them. And she reminded her grandparents of her good sense and honesty.

Her grandparents began to relax a little when they saw that Megan was taking responsibility for her own safety. They agreed to meet a few of her friends. And they promised to discuss some other ideas with her parents before they made any decision. Megan felt they were now more likely to say yes than no—and she was so glad!

Megan's grandparents found it easier to accept suggestions, rather than criticism, from their granddaughter. They appreciated her attitude and the respectful manner she used to talk with them.

You'll probably find this works with most of the adults in your life, as well. Suppose your basketball team is losing at half time and you think the coach should try a new play. You could yell at the coach, "You're fighting a losing battle! Move Chris over to defense, quick!" How do you think the coach would react?

Or you could speak to him quietly at half time, like this: "I have an idea that you might find useful. Maybe you could put Chris on defense to cover that team's tallest player." Do you think the coach would have a different reaction now? Why?

Sometimes people criticize to make themselves feel better. You probably know a person like this, someone who has something bad to say about everybody. She may act this way because deep inside, she wonders if she is as good as other people. When she finds fault in others, she feels relieved. This criticism is not helpful to anyone.

Before you criticize, take a moment to think. Why am I saying this? Can this be helpful to the other person? Am I just trying to hurt or embarrass the person? Once you understand your motives, you'll find it easier to choose your words.

Even when you're really trying to help, you may sometimes be surprised to find that the other person doesn't want your ideas. This may have nothing to do with you. Some people just won't accept *anybody's* suggestions. They want to learn alone and make their own mistakes.

BUILDING RESPECT

You'll find adults will give you more of their time and energy when they believe in you. It takes time to build a good relationship with the important people in your life. Unfortunately, it doesn't take long to destroy the respect and trust that you've worked so hard to gain.

Respect is an attitude that says, "you're an important person." When you tell the truth, act maturely, listen carefully, and choose your words well, you're showing respect. And 99 percent of the time, when you give respect, you get respect back.

Most good relationships are based on giving and receiving respect and trust. It's hard for you to believe someone who has lied to you. And when you don't tell the truth, it's hard for other people

ANNE CANEVARI GREEN 89

to believe you. It may take a long time before they trust you again. You'll need to show these people that you're reliable and honest.

But even if you've made mistakes in the past, you're older now and you can change. It's a good time to improve yourself and your relationships.

LEARNING TO COMPROMISE

Four-year-olds Jeannie, Brianne, and Kelly were all playing with Kelly's ball. They couldn't agree on which game to play; Jeannie wanted to play catch, Brianne wanted to play "hit the penny," and Kelly wanted to play "monkey in the middle." None of the girls would play what the other one wanted. They fought and shouted about it. Finally Kelly just picked up her ball and went home.

These little girls haven't learned how to compromise. When you compromise, you settle a problem by finding a solution that everyone can agree with.

Usually when you compromise, neither person gets exactly what he or she wants. They work out an agreement that will satisfy both.

There are some young people who treat their parents, teachers, and other adults like "the enemy." They scream and fight with them every chance they get. Do you think this behavior will earn them respect from the adults?

You have to expect some conflict with adults. After all, you don't always see eye-to-eye with your friends. All relationships have rough spots. Your friends have needs and desires which change. These may clash with your needs and desires. To keep your friendship intact, you've learned to compromise. This is a major step toward joining the adult world.

You've actually been practicing this since you were a toddler. Many times you'd ask your mother for some cookies and she'd tell you, "After lunch." Then you might ask, "Just one little one, *please?*" And if you had just the right expression on your face, you got your cookie.

As you enter your teenage years, you'll find it's helpful to compromise. You'll need patience and good communication skills to help you negotiate with the adults around you. You may not get what you want. But adults will tell you they don't get what they want all the time—or even most of the time—either.

Learning to compromise doesn't make you a loser. A successful compromise makes both people winners. And by accepting the compromise, you are showing respect and maturity.

Andrea wanted to wear makeup to the graduation dance. She had been talking to her mother about it since April. Many of her friends already wore lipstick to school every day. But Andrea's mother thought she was too young.

Andrea decided to have a serious talk with her mother just before the dance. She explained that she wanted her mother to trust her, so she didn't want to disobey her. But she also told her mother that many of the girls went to school without makeup and put it on at school. Then they wiped it all off on the school bus on the way home. Andrea didn't feel right about this idea. She wanted to discuss a compromise.

Her mother was very impressed with Andrea's honesty. She knew how hard it was to resist peer pressure in school. But she didn't want Andrea wearing makeup at such a young age. Finally she agreed to let her daughter wear lipstick, but only to the dance.

This made Andrea feel better. She didn't want to lie to her parents, but she did want to feel grown up and wear cosmetics. Andrea realized that once her mother thought about it, she might be able to get permission to wear lipstick or other makeup more often. They worked out a compromise that made sense to both of them, without fighting or leaving bad feelings.

ONWARD TO YOUR FUTURE

The next few years of your life will be packed full of new experiences. You'll be busy with school, friends, and family. You'll face some serious challenges, like decisions about alcohol, drugs, and sex. In the middle of all this, you'll be growing and changing.

You're polishing your personality and personal values. What kind of person do you want to be? This is a good time to take steps toward becoming the kind of person you can respect and admire. It's a good time to look at your goals and decide how you can work toward them.

No matter where your life leads you, you'll find it helpful and very rewarding to have good relationships with the people around you. Try out some of the ideas and tips we've outlined in this book. With a little practice, you'll find yourself more confident and better prepared to deal with the adults you know right now.

Even when things don't turn out the way you've planned, you can still hold your head up. Just live your life the best way you can, with self-respect and honor. Observe, learn, and improve yourself, and you'll be ready to function as a mature adult in your own exciting future.

FOR FURTHER READING

Berry, Joy. *Every Kid's Guide to Understanding Parents.* Chicago: Children's Press, 1987.

Blume, Judy. *Are You There God? It's Me, Margaret.* New York: Bradbury Press, 1970.

Cleary, Beverly. *Fifteen.* New York: Dell, 1980.

Cohen, Daniel and Susan Cohen. *Teenage Stress.* New York: M. Evans, 1984.

Collins, Gary R. *Changes: Becoming the Best You Can Be.* Granville, Ohio: Quest International, 1985.

Elchoness, Monte. *Why Can't Anyone Hear Me?* Sepulveda, California: Monroe Press, 1986.

Fitzpatrick, Regina. *It Wasn't the Truth They Told.* Nashville: Winston-Derek, 1988.

Griffith, Helen. *Journal of a Teenage Genius.* New York: Greenwillow, 1987.

Holland, Isabelle. *Now is Not Too Late.* New York: Lothrop, 1980.

Holman, Felice. *Slake's Limbo.* New York: Macmillan, 1986.

Johnson, Eric. *How to Live with Parents & Teachers.* Louisville, Kentucky: Westminster John Knox, 1986.

Kaufman, Stephen. *Does Anyone Here Know the Way to Thirteen?* Boston: Houghton Mifflin, 1985.

Killien, Christi. *Putting On An Act.* Boston: Houghton Mifflin, 1986.

LeShan, Eda. *When Grownups Drive You Crazy.* Boston: Little, Brown, 1988.

————. *You & Your Feelings: Understanding the Ups and Downs of Adolescence.* New York: Macmillan, 1975.

Marsh, Carole. *Meet in the Middle: The Parents Test—The Kids Test.* New York: Macmillan, 1983.

Miles, Betty. *Looking On.* New York: Avon, 1986.

Naylor, Phyllis. *Getting Along in Your Family.* Nashville: Abingdon, 1976.

Powledge, Fred. *You'll Survive: Problems of Adolescence.* New York: Macmillan, 1986.

INDEX